Copyright Notice

First Printing, 2013
ISBN-13: 978-1490390550
ISBN-10: 1490390553

Printed in the United States of America

TABLE OF CONTENTS

A BIT ABOUT ME

Thanks for taking the time to look at my book 'Cat Care: How to look after and care for your cat and kitten', I really appreciate it.

You might wonder who I am and what gives me the right to tell you how to look after your cat. My name is Sally Davis and I got my first cat, a British Short Haired named Josie, when I was just six years old. I will never forget going to the shelter with my parents and seeing all those wonderful cats, all shapes and sizes and all looking for a loving home. Josie stood out from the other cats because she seemed so confident, friendly and she had the most beautiful coat of fur I had ever seen. She soon became a member of the family and lived a very long and happy life with us.

I was just a girl then but my love for cats has grown and grown. I've owned and bred cats for most of my adult life. I currently live with two lovely boys; a set of regal Ragdolls called Paulie and Billy. I couldn't imagine life without them, and I hope they feel the same way about me!

My many years of cat loving have brought me to writing this book. If you're thinking about getting a cat or kitten, or already have one and want to understand everything about these beautiful creatures then this is for you!

I would like to take you on this journey with me as help you choose the right cat and explain how to cat-proof your home. I fully explain all elements of cat behaviour and even offer advice about preventing behavioural problems. I also speak in detail about health concerns; conditions your pet may be susceptible to, what the symptoms are, and of course what type of treatment is necessary.

Thanks again and enjoy!

Sally Davis

CHOOSING YOUR CAT AND MAKING HIM FEEL AT HOME

There are a few things you have to consider when looking for a new cat. Cats are complex creatures and other than being various colours and breeds, you have to consider the different behaviours and temperaments different felines exhibit. Allow me explain what you should look at when choosing a cat as well as the various places you should check out to find your ideal pet. Firstly I will tell you why Cats are the best.

Why get a cat?

Companionship: Cats are amazing company; scientists have proven that having a pet cat can reduce stress, help us relax and even recover from illnesses. Cats have a very therapeutic, calming and tranquil influence on people. From the sound of his purr to the warmth of his hair as he rubs against you it's a beautiful think to have a cat around.

Cat's are naturally independent animals and don't really need people or any other animals for that matter. Their self reliant nature means they're quite low maintenance compared to say dogs. As long as you feed him, give him some attention when he needs it, and make sure he has toys to occupy himself then he'll see you as mum, dad and best friend all rolled into one!

Daily care: Cat's have very few daily needs; you won't have to groom and clean him very often. Cats obsessively clean themselves so you will only really need to bathe him if he's absolutely filthy. The only thing you'll have to do is brush him every now and again or more frequently if he's long haired but this is a simple and quick task and one that many owners actually enjoy.

Exercise: You won't have to take your cat for a walk on a cold Tuesday morning when you just want to stay in bed; he can go outside and exercise himself and then get back in through the cat flap so you don't even need to go downstairs and let him in. Brilliant. Obviously playing with your cat will keep him fit and he will enjoy spending time with you; it just means if you leave him some toys and things to occupy himself with then he will do his own work out.

Other advantages: Cats eat very little, they don't bark, howl and wake the neighbourhood up at three in the morning. He might need a bit of daily attention but so what? What better feeling is there than a cat on your knee and a book in your hand? You can also usually pick up a fantastic cat for a small amount of money or even for free from some animal shelters and charities, some already neutered so the cost of adopting one is absolutely minimal.

Older or younger cat?

Would you prefer an adult cat or a kitten? An adult cat will be cheaper and already neutered. Although they'll have their own personalities you will still be able to connect with your cat and make him love you. A kitten is more demanding and will require extra care and attention but the advantage is if you raise him well then he won't suffer from behavioural problems and his personality will reflect the way you bring him up.

Colour

Cats come in all sorts of amazing colours, black, white, brown, and ginger. Some cats are single coloured, some multi-coloured. Although you will love your cat whatever he looks like there are many varieties in the natural world.

Shorthair or longhair?

Longhairs will require frequent grooming unless you want cat hairs all over your living room. You won't face as much of an issue with shorthaired cats although they will still need to be groomed on occasion.

Types of cat

Pure-bred: Bred from the same breed of pedigree parents. It will be easier to guess what the cat's personality and behaviour will be like when it grows up. These cats come in many different types and colours and are usually very carefully raised therefore they should be healthy and less prone to behavioural problems.

These are the most expensive types of cats however, and very rare ones might be difficult to get hold of. They also have a bigger chance of suffering from hereditary problems and certain ailments.

Cross-breed: Bred from pedigree parents, but of different breeds. The cat could grow to look like either parent or a mixture of both. These cats are less expensive than pure-breds, and if you know what type of cats the parents are like in terms of appearance and personality then it's an indication of what your cat will be like.

Non-pedigree: This means at least one of the cat's parents was cross-bred. Various breeds have been mixed over the generations making it harder to predict the temperament of the offspring and what they will look like. These cats can be very cheap or even free and are easily obtainable.

Sadly non-pedigree cats are not always treated the best so be aware of potential behavioural problems or ill health.

The right cat for you?

You have to look after your cat for its whole life, so this could be 15 years and in some cases cats live well into their 20's. With this considered you have to be aware that different cats have different needs. If you choose a boisterous, playful Tom then you will need to make time each day to play with him and give him the attention he craves. If you have a long-haired cat you will need to make sure you have the time to groom it on a regular basis.

Male or female?

Both males and females can make great pets but to prevent an unwanted litter you must ensure your cat is neutered when it reaches sexual maturity.

Unneutered males can be quite troublesome because they will tend to spray urine in the house in an attempt to attract a mate. They will also be more likely to stray and disappear for days on end looking for females.

Unneutered females can also cause problems. When their on heat they will become restless and make loud caterwauling sounds. They may also become very needy with their owners and require much more attention than a neutered feline.

Finding a nice cat

There are loads of places you can find yourself a lovely cat.

Breeder: Make sure you pick one that seems outgoing, lively and healthy. Confidence is another good quality of a cat. If it has all these characteristics then it's less likely to get unwell and will be more affectionate and fun to be around.

Newspaper or similar advert: Be aware of people trying to give cats away for free or on the cheap. You might find yourself a winner but then again you don't know anything of its medical history. Again make sure it looks healthy, confident and outgoing before you consider taking it home.

Cat charity or shelter: You can find yourself a fantastic cat at one of these. The shelter will have neutered the cats and they will be looking for a great new home which you can provide!

Friends or family: If you are offered a fabulous cat by friends and family then go for it. They are more likely to make you aware of any medical problems than if responding to an advert from a stranger.

What will your cat need when he moves in?

Litter tray: This will be used every day, probably on more than one occasion so it's vital you have it ready, one for each cat if you have more than one pet, so there's no arguing over territory. If possible find out what kind of tray the cat was using before and buy the same one. Make sure the tray is big enough for your cat and deep enough because cats like to bury their deposits in the litter. Put it on some old sheets of newspaper in case there's any spillage. You can get a covered litter tray which gives the cat its privacy and hides the contents from view. Some cats don't like these and feel claustrophobic and they're also quite dark which the cat might not like. An open tray is another option and despite the contents being on display as long as you clean up after the cat it won't be a problem and is the cheaper option.

Cat litter: There are several different types of litter available in shops. It's best to keep on using the same type because cats get used to the smell and feel of it and may refuse to use the tray if you suddenly change. If you do decide to change then do it gradually.

Clay litter is very cheap and probably the most common. This is generally very absorbent and you can even buy it scented to help disguise the smell.

Wood or paper litter is more expensive but is more effective at absorbing odours. If you're going to be out of the house and don't want to come back to a stink then this type will help reduce it.

Crystals: Very absorbent and are made to absorb liquid without clumping making for an easier clean-up. This kind of litter can be a bit more expensive.

Cat carrier: For when you go to the cattery, the vets, or to visit family or go on holiday the right cat carrier is essential. I wouldn't use a cardboard one because they aren't very secure and an able adult cat could easily find its way out. Cats don't like metal ones because of comfort issues and they're also quite heavy. You should go for a plastic one with a grill front door so the cat can see where he's going. It's also important because the cat has fresh air and light can get in. Make sure its sturdy, well-designed and easy for you to carry around. You could also put an old garment on the floor for extra comfort.

Bear in mind that if you're buying a carrier for a kitten then get a large enough one for an adult cat because he will grow! Like with the litter tray each cat should have his own carrier and they shouldn't be made to share.

Bedding: You can improvise and use many things for this. As long as it's comfy and soft your cat will love it. Things like cushions and pillows or you could even buy your cat a small bed from a pet shop. Don't forget to clean it every so often to help stop fleas. Each cat should have his own bed or designated sleeping place.

Cat flap: Don't forget that you will need to consider installing one of these as the cat gets older and wants to explore the great outdoors by himself.

Scratching posts: You will get one of these if you want you want to keep your expensive curtains looking nice! All cats love to scratch, anything and everything they can get their claws on. It's just a natural instinct and besides allowing them to shed the sheaths of their claws, it gives your cat a good old stretch. Scratching posts are available at all pet shops and each cat should have their own. They're mostly wooden with a carpeted covering. Make sure the post has a wide base, especially if you have a strong looking cat so it can't knock it over. Also make sure its high enough that your cat can stand on his back feet and still reach up and have a jolly good scratching session. I'd consider putting the post next to where your cat sleeps if possible, they tend to wake up and require a scratch. If you have a big house and your cat likes to wander about then put a few up in different rooms. If the post becomes worn out through relentless constant scratching then don't forget to replace it with a new one.

Toys: You will need to get your cat a variety of toys. Most cats love to have a play and it's nice and rewarding for you to play together. Cat toys are very cheap so it won't be expensive to entertain. Cats go crazy for catnip mice and little plastic balls; you could also consider battery operated mice and birds. Don't forget to make sure the toys are safe for your cat. Make sure there aren't any small parts which could easily come off and be chewed on or swallowed, never buy anything which looks small enough to go down your cats throat. Don't let it play with plastic bags; it could suffocate if the bag somehow went over its head or round its throat. Other simple ideas are balls of paper and cardboard boxes, all cats love sitting in boxes for some reason and this is guaranteed to keep him amused for a while.

Make sure you introduce new toys into playtime and rotate the old ones to make sure your cat doesn't get bored. If you leave him home alone keep the toys out so he can stay entertained until you get back. Playing with your cat is great fun and will help develop a loving bond between you so enjoy!

Collar: Get your cat a nice and soft collar and ID tag. You can engrave or write on your contact details. Most cats will scratch at their necks when you first put it on but they'll quickly get used to it so don't worry. Make sure the collar has suitable elasticity just in case it gets caught on anything and make sure you don't fasten it too tightly.

Microchip: The modern cat owner now uses a microchip to identify their cat. The vet can implant your pet with one from the age of 8 weeks onwards and this means if it's ever lost and taken to an animal rescue centre then they can scan the cat, identify its owners and return it to its rightful home.

Grooming supplies: Make sure you get a special brush designed for cats if your pet is long-haired. Even if it isn't its worth investing in a brush to stop hair getting everywhere.

BRINGING YOUR CAT HOME FOR THE FIRST TIME

Right, so you've chosen yourself a fantastic cat and you've purchased the latest in high-tech cat toys. You've got some sexy scratching posts and a diamond encrusted litter tray; now let me go through a few steps you should take to make sure your new cat's transition to his new home runs as smoothly as possible.

Make sure you have lots of spare time when first bringing your cat home, especially if he's a kitten. Your pet might be a little nervous or unconfident in his new surroundings so make sure you show him round the house and let him know that it's safe. Show your cat where his food and water is, where his bed is and where his litter tray and scratching posts are. To ease the cat into the new environment you could consider putting all its things in one private room for a few days to give it time to acclimatise and relax. If you don't have a spare room then set your pet aside a very clear territory for all his things.

When it comes to finally driving him home, make sure you fasten the cat carrier with a seatbelt securely in the back seat. If he starts to cry don't let him out of the carrier, just speak to him in a soft reassuring manner and let him know everything's ok and you'll be home soon. Don't forget to drive safely and not to brake too harshly if you can help it.

When you finally arrive home let him into his own room or private area and just leave him for an hour or so. He might be stressed at the move so it's best to leave him by himself for a while so he can compose himself and get used to his surroundings. After a while let him out and let him explore and investigate his new home. If you have children make sure they aren't too loud and don't expect him to play right away. Stroke him gently and speak softly and reassuringly, this will help him settle in.

Don't let your cat out the house for at least 2 weeks or even longer depending on the cat. If after 2 weeks he still seems nervous and unsettled then bear with him for a while longer. Some cats just take longer to adapt to new surroundings, so don't worry too much. Others are more laid back and settle in much quicker.

FEEDING YOUR CAT

We all know cats love a good meal. As his owner, you'll be responsible for keeping him healthy and giving him the balanced diet he requires to ensure a long and happy life! Below I will list the components of a balanced diet.

Proteins: Meat contains proteins, amino acids and enzymes which are essential to your cat. Protein helps build the body and repair body tissue. It also helps growth and regulates his metabolism. Taurine is the amino acid which is most important to your cat. A taurine deficiency could cause nervous system disorders, heart disease, arrested growth and even death in some circumstances. Whatever food you buy make sure it contains taurine, I cannot emphasise this enough. Most good brands will contain it but not all so make sure you double check.

Carbohydrates and fats: Carbs fuel your cat's body and give him energy to do his cat activities. They also add much needed fibre to the diet. If you administer a low fat diet for your kitten then it will seriously impair his growth rate and make his coat look dull and dry.

Vitamins and minerals: Antioxidants vitamins A, C and E strengthen the immune system and can reduce the chances of your cat getting certain cancers. Amazingly cats create their own vitamin C so you won't have to force-feed your new pet a lemon. Vitamin A helps maintain good eye-sight and vitamin E helps organ and muscle functions. Vitamin D is vital for maintaining healthy teeth and bones. The various B vitamins are good for maintaining a healthy coat, skin and general growth. Most good quality pre-prepared cat foods will contain all these vital vitamins and minerals making it easier for you to provide your pet with a balanced diet.

Just looking at the cat food section at your local supermarket might be a daunting prospect. This coupled with the multitude of adverts we see on TV and billboards these days maybe the source of some confusion. Don't let it be! As long as it's a good quality brand you'll be ok.

A kitten will need around twice as many calories as an adult cat; they also need more protein, vitamins, fats and taurine. For this reason most good supermarkets and pet shops sell 'Kitten Formula' which as the name suggests provides all the nutrition your kitten will need until he reaches adulthood.

I will now explain the different cat foods available on the market.

Pre-prepared: These are the most common cat foods you see in supermarkets. The packaging might all look similar with a picture of a healthy looking cat chomping away; but don't be mislead. Cheap, low-end products often contain lots of sugar, salt and preservatives which won't provide a balanced diet and the right nutrients for your pet.

Middle ranged and priced products are obviously better than cheaper ones and provide all the ingredients to ensure a balanced and healthy diet. The only problem is these kinds often contain meat or animal by-products, left over bits and pieces which are not the best quality. By-products could be a tasty mixture of bones, skin and organs, so before you choose to buy these products, be aware that you can't be certain what you're feeding him.

Premium expensive cat foods are made with better ingredients. They contain less preservatives, sugars, salt and colouring and are made from actual meat and not meat by-products. These might not be available at your typical supermarket so try your local pet shop. Middle ranged foods are perfectly fine for your cat it's just premium brands are another option.

Pre-prepared food comes wet, dry and semi-moist. Try the different types out and see what your cat likes best.

Canned food: Wet food. Can be eaten alone or with dry food. Remember to check the nutritional information and make sure there aren't too many colourings, preservatives, salt and sugar. Canned food is the healthiest type but don't forget to throw away uneaten food and cover and refrigerate anything that's left in the container.

Dry food: Only buy dry food that contains meat and not meat by-products. Dry food usually has a long shelf life but despite of this make sure you store it in an airtight plastic container. Dry food is good because you can leave it out all day and it won't spoil, so if you're out for the day always choose this option.

Semi-moist food: This contains lots of preservatives so never consider it as the main staple of your cat's diet. It also contains many chemicals and colourings and I recommend only using it when you're faced with no other choice.

Feeding schedule

There are two kinds of ways you can feed your pet. Self-feeding is where you will leave some dry food out for your cat and he will just help himself throughout the day. This is more practical if you're out at work during the day and can't be at home. The problem with this is that cats have very little impulse control when it comes to feeding and it's likely he will overeat and become overweight if you employ this as a long term strategy. If you leave him some food and go away for a day it's also likely he'll just eat it all in one sitting so there's nothing left for later on.

The ideal option is regular feeding when obviously you're around and can feed your cat according to his usual schedule. Make sure you try and stick to the expected schedule to avoid upsetting your pet. Scheduled feeding is better because it ensures your cat won't overeat and therefore has a more balanced and healthier diet. Don't feel too bad if you have to leave him for a few days and entrust him to self-feed and don't forget you could always ask a friend or neighbour to pop in and give him his dinner!

How much to feed your cat

Below are the recommended feeding amounts based on the age of the cat

Kittens 8-12 weeks: 5 meals a day consisting of 25g (1oz)

Kittens 12-20 weeks: 4 meals a day.

Kittens 20-30 weeks: 3 meals a day.

Adolescents 30 weeks-1 year: 2 meals a day

Adult 1 year-8years: 1 or 2 meals a day

Old age 8 years plus: 1 or 2 meals a day

These are just rough feeding guidelines based upon my many years of breeding and raising cats but you also have to take into consideration the cat's age, weight and level of activity. For example a house cat will not need as many calories as a playful Tomcat that goes round chasing dogs all day. The above amounts are based upon a cat of average size and activity levels.

GROOMING YOUR CAT

You will play an essential role in the grooming of your cat, help him looking good and staying healthy. This won't take long and is actually one of the most enjoyable parts of the relationship between me and my cats!

Brushing: It's better to start getting your cat used to brushing as soon as you bring him home simply to accustom him to it quicker. As I mentioned earlier brushing and combing is very important especially with long-haired breeds. Cats are constantly growing new hair at a rapid rate and losing old hairs just as quickly. Severe shedding may be a sign of an emotional or medical problem. If your cat is over grooming and pulling lumps out of his own fur then take him to the vet. Long-haired cats will need grooming daily and short-haired breeds will need attention twice a week.

Brushing and combing is essential because it reduces the amount of hair the cat swallows when he self-cleans. This is good because it cuts down the chances of him developing hairballs, constipation or even intestinal blockages. If your cat ever starts to choke up its own hair then don't worry, this is just a natural reaction to stop him swallowing too much.

Before brushing make sure you untie any tangles in the cat's fur with your fingers (This will be more relevant to long-haired breeds) Start with the head, use gentles strokes in the direction that the fur lies (cats strongly dislike their hair being brushed in the opposite way to which it grows) and make your way down its body, sides and legs. Keep checking the brush and when you've collected a lot of hair then make sure you remove it before proceeding. You may have to repeat this process until you get rid of all the loose fur. In my experience as long as you're gentle then most cats really enjoy a good brush because it's a similar method to stroking. I find it relaxing and therapeutic so I'm not sure who enjoys it more!

Bathing: No this is not a joke. I have been bathing cats for decades. It's true that cat's saliva contains a cleaning agent and for the most part they are quite capable of cleaning themselves but there are some exceptions. If he gets really muddy or puts his feet in wet cement or something then he will need a proper wash. This is perfectly safe you just need to invest in a cat or kitten shampoo which can be bought at most good pet shops; these don't contain the same chemicals as products designed for humans.

Cats can actually swim but they will generally show aversion to being bathed so make sure you follow these steps. First of all he is to be bathed in the kitchen sink and not in the bath. Fill the sink with a few inches of tepid water and rub a little shampoo into the fur. Avoid getting any in the cat's eyes, ears or mouth. If he does try to resist then it's ok to hold him securely as long as you're not hurting him, this is a short process and won't last long. Rinse the fur thoroughly with cupfuls of water until all the shampoo has gone from his fur. Dry him off with a towel and then keep him indoors to recover. You should give him some attention or a treat to show how good he was. If you do this then its increasingly more likely that he'll be slightly more tolerant when it next comes to bath-time!

Eye care: Cats sometimes gather sleep or residue in the corner of their eyes. This can be gently wiped off with a wet cotton ball. If he develops a serious eye problem and it looks red or infected then take him to the vet immediately and don't attempt to treat it yourself because cat's eyes are extremely sensitive.

Nail care: Most owners don't clip their cat's nails, it's not essential and regular use of scratching posts will take care of them in a natural way. If you decide you want to then you need to buy a special clipper designed for cutting cat's nails. He may resist because cats don't like their feet being touched but if you gently press down on them then he should extend his claws and you can proceed. The more times you cut his nails the more used to it he will get and the easier it will be. Make sure you only trim the white tip (1/8 to 1/4 of an inch) or (0.3 to 0.6 cm) and not the pink part of the nail which is where the blood vessels and nerves are so be very careful. As I said a cat will get used to this procedure over time if he's young but if you introduce an older cat to it then he could be more resistant. If this happens consider taking him to the vet for advice or employ a professional groomer.

Ear care: You won't have to spend much time worrying about this but I thought it would be worth mentioning anyway. If you look inside your cat's ears and you seen waxy deposits then action can be taken. This could be a result of mites or an ear infection and in this case take him to the vet. To help prevent any of these instances it's quick and easy to clean your cat's ears. Simply clean out the ears with a cotton ball dipped in baby oil until they look clean. Your cat may not like this so remember to hold him securely but gently if he starts to resist and don't feel bad because you're doing this for his own good.

Dental care: Good dental care is very important and can reduce future vet bills because it can help prevent gum disease, bad breath, tooth loss and the build up of plaque. Like with the other grooming procedures its best to start when the cat's at a young age so he gets used to it quickly. Like with nail care for adult cats if he is too resistant then you will have to take him to a vet. I usually brush my cats teeth once a week, so make sure you buy a cat toothbrush and some cat toothpaste (Don't use human toothpaste, it'll make him sick and he prefers cat flavours like chicken and beef anyway) Firstly you need to open his mouth. If you gently tilt his head back the mouth should open. Healthy teeth will be intact and all there! Healthy gums will be pink. If the gums are bleeding or swollen and the teeth cracked or missing then you need to take your pet to the vet.

Brush the teeth gently one row at a time. You only need to do the outside fortunately because the cat cleans the insides himself. Don't forget you don't need to rinse the mouth with water afterwards because cat toothpaste is edible and I'm sure he'll quite like the taste. Your pet might resist to start with but once he realises how delicious the toothpaste is he should relax for you!

Getting a professional groomer: If you have money to spare this could be an option. A professional groomer will look after all your cats grooming needs including hair, nails and teeth without you ever having to stress about it. You will be able to find a decent one from a simple Google search, asking around other cat owners or from asking at your local cattery.

Overall I really enjoy grooming time with my cats. I've done it since they were all kittens so they're used to it by now. Remember its normal for your cat to resist and exhibit some discomfort initially but this will stop the longer you do it and you'll find many cats actually enjoy it. Just make sure you're gentle and you talk to your cat in a soothing voice if he starts to look stressed, and don't forget to give him a treat as a reward for good behaviour once you've finished. In the natural world adult cats groom their own kittens so this is just an extension of that really. Good luck and have fun bonding together!

CAT BEHAVIOUR

Cats get on pretty well with humans and often develop a loving affectionate relationship with people if they're treated nicely. If you make the effort to learn and understand what your cat is communicating to you then you will have a better indication of what he needs. The behaviour of cats is an interesting and complex subject and demonstrates how intelligent they really are. The next section I attempt to explain most types of behaviour helping you know what your pet needs.

MARKING, SCRATCHING AND RUBBING

Scent marking: Scent marking is very important in the world of cats and plays a vital part in maintaining distance and avoiding inter-cat aggression. Cats will deposit what are called scent signals, produced by special scent producing glands on their bodies. These glands are found on the face, paws and the base of the tail. Scent signals are deposited to identify the cat to other felines and communicate with them how long he's been in the area. This marking of territory serves to avoid the inter-cat aggression I mentioned.

Cats decode these signals via not only smell but also taste. What happens relates to the Jacobson's organ, which is located in the hard palette and accessed by two small openings in the mouth. These openings lead to two fluid-filled sacs lined with olfactory (scent) cells. Scent is then forced up into these ducts when the cat presses his tongue into the roof of his mouth.

To do this the cat engages in the Flagmen reaction which you might recognise. This is characterised by the stretching of neck, opening of mouth and wrinkling of nose to produce what looks like a snarl. This is perfectly normal, nature taking its course so please don't be alarmed and think your pet's having a seizure!

These signals are imperceptible to humans and cats have a much heightened sense of smell and taste so are able to use scent marking as a form of communication.

Scratching: A cat clawing at the garden shed or a fence might be a common site but the common nature of this action belies its complexity in regard to the cat communication it actually demonstrates. Most people think that first and foremost cats scratch for fun, or to sharpen their claws; but in reality it's done to remove the blunted outer claw sheath to reveal a brand new sharper version underneath.

Cats also scratch as part of their exercise regime and to strengthen the muscles and tendons. You will probably now notice your cat scratching loads! This is very important to keep his claws as sharp and strong as possible. Cats traditionally need sharp claws for killing prey, fighting and climbing. Even though your cat will be domesticated and won't necessarily need to catch prey and involve himself in confrontations it's simply an inherited predilection.

Marking is a less known reason for scratching. The paws contain scent glands so when a cat marks a surface then it's letting other cats in the neighbourhood know who he is.

Rubbing: Cats like rubbing their faces on things. To the untrained eye it just looks like it feels nice, I don't doubt that it does but it's not the primary reason they do it! Cats leave scent signals on various objects using the scent glands on their faces. They are leaving cat messages for other felines and reassuring themselves that their territory is safe and secure for them to be happy in.

My cats always rub my legs when they see me and stick their tails upright. This is a greeting gesture and shows the affection my pets have for me. Even though they've been doing it all their lives I still find it really cute.

Cats rub each other sometimes, although this is usually instigated by the physically weaker animal and is a tool to acknowledge status amongst felines.

Urine marking: Spraying urine is another way in which cats communicate and must be differentiated from when he's just drank too much cream and needs to go to the toilet.

Cats can deposit sprays of urine whatever they feel like it regardless of how much liquid is in their bladder. They usually stand when making these deposits because if they're left near nose height then other cats will be able to detect them easier. Regardless of a cat being neutered, urine spraying is an important inter-cat communication method and is utilised by both sexes equally. Cats are usually very private about going to the toilet and if they need to go outside they will retire behind a bush or somewhere secluded. If a cat brazenly urinates in the open then that is a sign that he wants to communicate.

Urine marking of outdoor territory is done to make sure the area isn't over saturated with unfamiliar cats. If a female does it then she is showing signs that she may be ready to mate. This sexually-related spraying will be accompanied by various cat noises to make clear their intentions. Of course neutered cats will not have this natural impulse so won't do it, but I wanted to let you know what one of the biological reasons was.

Before people understood cats properly they thought that urine spraying was an act of aggression threatening other cats not to encroach on their territory. Experts now understand that they aren't aggressive and other cats are drawn to them and have a sniff with great interest. Some cats will deposit some urine in the same place as a friendly 'I'm in the area too'. Unconfident, insecure cats are also known to do it because they want to spread their personal odour around and get more confident.

The most uncommon form of marking is Middening and this is the deliberate depositing and leaving of faeces marking off the boundaries of a cats territory. He is saying in no uncertain terms that this patch is taken; no one else is welcome so get lost!

SOCIALISING

It's interesting to learn about how cats socialise with other cats, but also humans. Remember when you first bring your cat home to let him come to you rather than impose yourself on him. A cat might feel uneasy in a new environment so it's best to give him some time to do things at his own pace so he doesn't feel threatened. It's obviously easier to make friends with a cat if you feed him, play with him and generally treat him well.

If you look after your pet well and bring him up with love and affection in a safe and secure home then he'll grow up to be friendly and sociable and will be less likely to suffer from behavioural problems. The amount of interaction a cat has as a kitten will determine how well he socialises with humans as an adult. As I keep saying if you want a human-friendly cat then all you need to do is take good care of him.

Despite what I have just said certain cats simply don't enjoy human companionship as well as others. Some cats prefer spending time alone or with other cats and au contraire some absolutely adore being constantly around humans. Some breeds are less social and it won't make for a harmonious and healthy relationship if you try and impose yourself too much on them. If you want a social cat make sure you choose a more friendly and gregarious breed.

There are other factors other than natural breed predilection that determine levels of socialisation. If a cat was mistreated as a kitten then it might tend to avoid humans. Cats are intelligent and will remember if people were mean to them but luckily they are also forgiving and you can slowly rebuild a cat's trust in people with love and caring.

You should also be aware of the impact any children can have on your cat. Children don't always respect their needs and can be too noisy, aggressive and rough. A tough Tomcat might be able to hold his own but the majority of cats would find this over the top. A child could quite unintentionally scare and cause great anxiety for a cat so if you have children then explain to them about how pets should be respected.

Believe it or not cats will generally get on well with other types of animals. It might sound bizarre but if you rub the cat with the bedding of say your pet rabbit then the scent will be transferred, the cat will get accustomed to the smell and therefore be more sociable towards the rabbit.

When your cat moves in don't introduce him to your other pets straight way, remember the settling in period is very important. If you have dogs, don't let them bark, growl and act excitedly towards your cat because this will frighten him. When the excitement of a cat being around fades then most dogs will usually simply forget about them and go about their daily business completely oblivious, potentially completely ignoring each other. Cats and dogs can live together in harmony but they're seldom best pals.

When two unfamiliar cats meet then it can take a while for them to get used to each other. This is completely normal so don't think it's weird they aren't hugging each other straight away like in pictures you see on the internet. It's best to supervise the initial meeting of two cats. They will usually begin proceedings by the rubbing of noses together and then there are many variables that can determine how it goes from here. If one cat is shy then he may walk away, if he's feeling brave then he might hiss, or if he's ambivalent he might just sniff the other cat. First meetings usually go more smoothly if the participants are of the opposite sex and are neutered. Even so In most cases cats are rarely hostile towards each other if they've been well socialised, and will invariably happily co-exist. The relationship between them that develops depends on several things including age, sex and personalities and I always find it fun watching how these funny little friendships evolve! Some cats will become mates quicker than they would with other cats, just like with people really. Eventually they will accept each other. Just don't forget to still pay attention to your original pet, this will reassure him that his position and status within the house remains and will make for a smoother inter-animal relationship

HUNTING

All cats hunt, even domesticated ones who eat expensive pet food and have their nails done weekly by a professional groomer. It has little to do with appeasing hunger and more to do with the hard-wired natural urge to hunt and kill prey. It is an inevitable truth of cat nature that they will hunt, just as they will walk and breath.

Rural cats tend to hunt the available pray in their local environment but urban cats scavenge for food left by humans. Domesticated pet cats just hunt for the excitement of the chase, capture and eventual kill of their unfortunate prey. They hunt for birds, rats, mice and other vermin in the UK. In warmer climes they even go after grasshoppers and scorpions.

Despite having senses that are optimised for hunting at night, a cat will hunt any time of day that takes his fancy. He will be attracted to an area by scent, for example detecting rat urine. He will then wait in the area until he locks onto the prey in his crosshairs. The cat will then pounce on its side with immense speed and athleticism and start to rake the prey with its hind claws while pinning it down with his forepaws. He will then put the prey out of its misery with a bite to the neck. The teeth slip exactly between the neck vertebrae and result in a highly efficient instant kill. Feral cats are usually better hunters because hunting is a simple tool to avoid starvation and so mastering the art is essential. Domestic cats don't have the same motives but their razor sharp teeth and clauses coupled with their lightening quick reactions means they are still a match for most small mammals.

A successful kill by a domesticated cat will be reacted to by a delighted display of rapturous jumping around. This self-celebratory display is seldom demonstrated by feral cats, probably because killing becomes so mundane and commonplace it doesn't have the novelty factor a domestic cat might enjoy.

Cats have to adopt a different hunting technique when preying on birds for obvious reasons. Birds can fly away so cats have to be even more careful when planning an attack. They will usually stalk in long grass to remain silent and unsighted and will remain very low, almost crawling and move forward with great care. When it gets close enough the cat jumps on his prey and there's only one outcome. A cat won't have any luck on a recently cut lawn because he has nowhere to hide!

Cats are responsible for many bird deaths worldwide. Recent estimates suggest as many as 55 million a year in the UK and a figure of over 3 billion in the US. Although hunting is natural and cats DNA is programmed to do it and always will be, I would still suggest reducing the amount of unnecessary deaths of prey. This can be done by simply buying a cat collar with a bell attached. Even the stealthiest cats in the world can't prevent that dastardly bell from ringing and scaring that mouse or bird away. Cats have a natural inclination to hunt, yes; but stopping him from being successful will not have a bad effect on your pet.

BODY LANGUAGE

A cat will rely greatly on body language to communicate his feelings. Feline body language is quite complicated and cats can demonstrate emotions such as sadness, fear, frustration and happiness. In this section I will attempt to deconstruct the major aspects of feline emotions so with practice and experience you're able to understand and interpret it fully.

Neutral: This is how most healthy cats spend most of their day. In a state of content, comfortable relaxation. If lying down he will be stretched out, curled up into a ball or lying on his front with his paws tucked underneath him. His eyes will be half closed and he may blink softly. His ears and whiskers will be relaxed, and it might actually look like he's smiling at you! He's not tense or uncomfortable and is happily just sat there chilling thinking his cat thoughts.

Happy: A happy cat is pretty obvious. Whilst sitting he will be relaxed and upright with his ears pointed forward and upwards. When lying down he will have his paws tucked underneath him or he may be lying stretched out on his side or back with his legs spread outwards. Cats don't expose their chests generally unless they feel totally at rest and happy so if he starts rolling over showing his belly then he's one happy cat. Like when a cat is in neutral mode his eyes might be closed or half-open. His tail will be still, or nice and upright if he's greeting you. Another tell-tale sign of catisfaction is if you stroke him and hear that familiar purr.

Angry: Hopefully your cat will never get in this state, but I thought it was necessary to detail all aspects of body language so I'm including this. You need to be very careful if faced with an angry cat. His body will be rigid and invariably his tail will be extended completely straight. In most circumstances he will be hiss, spit or make a very low growling sound. This may be allied with an attempt to look as big and threatening as possible with his erect fur and adopting a low crouching position with stiff front legs.

His ears will be flat against his head and his eyes will be focussed and concentrating, with the pupils narrowing to just a slit. The whiskers will also be stiff and held away from his face. If you have the misfortune to witness your cat in this state then whatever you do don't provoke him, even unintentionally. Don't stare or shout at him, make any sudden movements or even try to touch and comfort him.

It's best just to leave him alone and give him space until he calms down and composes himself. There's no reason why your cat should behave like this if you treat him well and keep him away from nasty dogs. If your cat suffers persistent angry episodes then I would suggest taking him to a vet.

Frustrated: Frustration in cats is divided into two types. Firstly and most seriously a long-term frustration born out of depression which happens due to a lack of stimulation e.g. He can't get outside for whatever reason so he can't fulfil his natural cat desires and likes such as hunting and running around outdoors. You can tell if a cat has this long-term frustrated depression if he becomes more withdrawn and less likely to want to play and socialise with humans and other cats. A cat in this condition might also start to eat less.

Secondly a cat might get frustrated as a result of a singular event e.g. he wants to reach a snack but can't. This is obviously less serious and will involve your pet completely focussing on the desired object. The eyes will be wide-open and pupils dilated, ears forward and whiskers spread and forward pointing. If he can't get what he wants he will pace around impatiently perhaps licking his lips in frustration. Rest assured if you simply give your cat the snack he will soon forget his stressed state and go back to his usual happy self.

Anxious. Anxious cat's eyes will be open wide and he won't blink. His pupils will dilate and the more anxious he is, the more flat his ears will become against his head. His head will usually lower and the whiskers may be swept forward in a state of alert or go down and pulled to the side in an attempt to make his face look as non-threatening and small as possible. If he gets more anxious he may cower in a corner or behind an object, it's very common for cats to start to arch their back too, adopting a position that would make running away easy. The tail can be still or moving slowly from side to side.

 The anxious body language is pretty slow and subtle so it will require careful observation to detect his mood. There's nothing to be alarmed about if your cat gets anxious from time to time. Females are generally more likely to get anxious but even the bravest Tomcat might get a bit anxious if he hears some loud fireworks. The best way to cure an anxious cat is to speak to him gently, show him some love and give him a good old stroke!

Scared: It's quite easy to identify fear and even a feline body language novice will recognise when a cat is scared. His ears will be flat against his head and this may be coupled with the head being lowered and an upwards looking stare. Obviously if a cat is scared he may just run away but if there isn't room to manoeuvre then he might just crouch and remain very still. His eyes will be wide open and fully focussed with fully dilated pupils and the whiskers will be flattened back. He may start to hiss, spit or even growl and extend his claws ready to strike out if he needs to. In a similar fashion to an angry cat he may attempt to make himself look as big as possible by fluffing up the fur and straightening the front legs. The back legs will remain in a crouched position ready to spring.

Like what I said about an angry cat, there is no reason why your cat should ever be especially fearful as long as you look after him and keep him away from aggressive dogs and other dangerous animals such as snakes. If your cat does ever get extremely fearful then he will only return to normality once he is satisfied the threat has fully disappeared, you won't be able to appease him straight away with a stroke and a catnip mouse.

Relieved: This is a change after a negative emotional state such as being scared or anxious. If you're able to identify relief in your cat then you'll realise he's over the particular trauma and is close to being his usual self. Feline relief will resonate all over his body. The whiskers will relax, the head will lower and the whole body just calms down as the negative emotional state is vanquished. He may also do a full body stretch and the half-closed eyes of a neutral or happy cat may return!

SLEEPING HABITS

Domestic cats sleep for about two thirds of their lives which equates to around 16 hours a day! They have body clocks that tend to wake them up in the early morning and at dusk when it's likely their prey will be most active.

They will be more likely to fit their catnaps in after exercise, a big meal or if they're in a comfortable and warm environment. Cats will also sleep when they are bored and have nothing to do; another reason why you should give your cat attention and make sure he has lots of toys to play with and exciting things to do.

Cats always amuse me in the way they can doze off almost anywhere and sometimes render the expensive bed you have just bought completely redundant. When a cat wants to sleep he will make it fairly obvious and it's best to leave him to it. Make sure he isn't sleeping somewhere unsafe or in a spot that is in the way of your everyday routine, try and coerce him into sleeping somewhere safe and out of the way from a young age so he sticks to it as he grows up.

Like humans a cats sleep pattern falls into two distinct phases; Rapid Eye Movement (REM) sleep and Non Rapid Eye Movement (Non REM) sleep. Unlike humans cats will alternate between dozing and a deeper sleep, each phase lasting less than thirty minutes. Cats will also have more regular but shorter periods of sleep spread out over the whole day rather than sleeping say 8 hours at a time as humans do. During REM sleep you might notice your cat might twitch his ears, whiskers and limbs; this is completely normal and doesn't suggest some kind of fit is imminent.

Scientists actually think that cats dream during REM sleep, not about human problems such as paying the bills and looking for a new job; but probably about a new scratching post or a particularly tasty bird that he saw in the garden earlier.

As your cat sleeps his head may be raised and his paws will be tucked neatly underneath him, perhaps even sitting up. This isn't a deep sleep and he's subconsciously aware of his surroundings and potential dangers in the area. He's sitting up so he can spring into action if he needs to. The funny thing is cats always wake up from this state in a hurry and stand to attention when they hear it's time for some food!

Non REM sleep is deeper and during this phase your cat is restoring his energy and his immune system is building up again. The posture is more relaxed and he will be lying on his side. After a nice deep sleep you will notice that a cat reacts in a very human-like manner; with blinking, stretching, yawning followed by a wash and a bit of grooming!

Kittens require lots of Non REM sleep because this is when they develop their muscles and bones ready for adulthood. Older cats are far less in need of deep sleep because they simply don't expend as much energy as their younger friends. Having said that, elderly cats still like to spend the day blissfully dozing away.

BEHAVIOURAL PROBLEMS

Just about all cats develop behavioural problems at some time in their life; the important thing to remember is that the problems I mention are not deliberately enacted just to annoy humans. Many behavioural 'problems' are just normal activity in a cat's mind and he won't realise he's doing anything 'wrong'. Luckily there are simple ways we can eradicate such issues.

SCRATCHING FURNITURE

This is a common problem millions of cat owners are subject to. Your cat doesn't have a problem with your taste in sofas or curtains he just sees it as something he can have a good old scratch on. To avoid having your furniture torn apart simply make sure you have a few scratching posts dotted about your pets usual haunts in the house. To encourage use of the scratching posts I suggest rubbing catnip on them and by rewarding use with food rewards, verbal praise and a nice stroking.

It's also an idea to make sure your cat has plenty of toys to play with in another attempt to divert his attention away from furniture. If you do catch your cat scratching furniture then don't be scared to shout 'No' at him or make a sudden deliberate noise, if you do this then he will learn to associate the telling off with his behaviour and he should stop eventually.

As a last resort you could simply keep your pet away from any rooms containing any expensive furniture, but from my experience you can reduce the whole dilemma to virtually zero by making sure he has enough toys, cardboard boxes and scratching posts to completely distract him.

DEFACATING OR URINATING IN THE HOUSE

Bad toilet behaviour is triggered be various things such as.

1: Your cat doesn't like where his litter tray is situated, maybe it's too close to his sleeping or eating areas.

2: His tray isn't cleaned often enough.

3: Your pet doesn't like to use the particular litter you buy.

4: The tray is too small and the litter not deep enough.

5: Some breeds will do this if they're separated from their owner for too long.

If you make sure to avoid the aforementioned problems then you can rest assured that your cat won't be surprising you with random presents in the hallway.

EATING HOUSEPLANTS

This can be a common problem and not only is it annoying having your beautiful plants nibbled on by your pet but it's also potentially dangerous as some plants are poisonous to cats. The likes of Ivy, Caladium, Philodendron and Sago palm are poisonous to cats and some are even deadly so it's worth having a look on Google for a more exhaustive list. Obviously the best thing to do would be to keep such plants out of your cats reach and bear in mind that cats are focussed and determined animals so they really should be physically impossible to get to. If you're still paranoid then simply get rid of them, it's not worth jeopardising your pet's health.

An alternative way to stop a cat munching on your prized plant life is to provide him with trays of seedling grass sprouts. These are sold specifically for this purpose and can be bought in most pet shops. The average feline will prefer to chew on these than your plant collection even when he has access to plants outside; nobody knows why I guess they just taste better!

SEPERATION FROM YOU

Some breed of cats especially Burmese and Siamese have a high need for attention and contact from their owners. They can become distressed and unsettled if they are left alone for too long. Unfortunately this anxiety can manifest into behavioural problems such as urinating and defecating in the home, cloth and wool sucking and even self-harm. This anxiety will only be arrested if you give him the attention he requires. If you know you're going to be out at work all day and have other engagements that mean you won't often be home and you don't have someone to look after your pet then you should avoid getting a Burmese or Siamese and go for a more independent type such as a Manx or a British shorthaired.

SUCKING AND EATING CLOTH AND OTHER MATERIALS

Many cats seem to enjoy eating and sucking cloth and all kinds of non-food objects. Obviously you could start to reduce this issue by removing problematic objects from the cat's vicinity. I used to have a cat named Percy and he started to suck on random clothes strewn about my house. I found that by giving him something more acceptable to suck and chew on such as a toy or the grass seedlings I mentioned previously it would appease his predilection for eating my best sweaters! You can even put bitter apple on items to suppress your pets sucking desires. Eventually he will associate the bad taste to chewing on non-food items and eventually stop. If he persists then please contact a vet because in some circumstances these suggestions won't work and your cat might need special medication.

OVER GROOMING

As I explained earlier in this book grooming is an important part of caring for your cat. Considering they can sleep up to 20 hours a day and don't have many worries bigger than what scratching post they should use, cats like humans can suffer from stress which can manifest into over grooming which can cause baldness and skin damage from excessive self-licking and chewing. If your cat shows symptoms of this excessive behaviour then please take him to see the vet. The vet will help you diagnose and thusly suggest treatment to relieve this condition. The main techniques to prevent over grooming are listed below.

1: If the reason is parasitic infection then medication will prevent it.

2: Anti anxiety and anti depression medication will prevent it if these are the reasons.

3: By keeping your cat's daily routine as similar as possible. Feed him, play with him and let him out at similar times each day. Cat's love routine and a clear-cut well-defined routine will make him less stressed and therefore less likely to over groom.

4: Make sure your pet has loads of toys, scratching posts and suchlike to occupy himself and prevent him from getting bored and depressed. Even consider a specially developed 'Cat video' that can be found online (have a look at 'Videos for cats' on YouTube) or getting a fish tank. Cats find these both very therapeutic and relaxing and are also much more economic than hiring a shrink.

Whatever you do don't punish your cat for over grooming or reward him for not doing it. This simply won't help and is best avoided.

AGGRESSION TOWARDS PEOPLE

Not all cats get aggressive but generally a lot will display such tendencies at some time. Females are less prone to be aggression to males, and non-neutered cats will be more aggressive than neutered ones. I will now try to explain the different kinds of aggression towards people and hopefully how you can reduce it.

Play-based aggression: This is common in young and active cats generally those less than three years old. When young cats play, chase things, bite them and pounce on them they are honing the predatory and survival skills that they would naturally have to utilise in the wild. Playful aggression can result in your cat biting and scratching your skin and can be quite annoying and unwarranted especially when you are minding your own business and he suddenly attacks you. This behaviour will obviously be encouraged if you tease him and invite him to chase and bite you but don't worry this behaviour is entirely natural and should start to decrease as your cat gets older and matures. The following steps will help you reduce your pet's aggressive behaviour towards you.

1: Make sure he has lots of toys, scratching posts and other things to keep him occupied with. An active cat that lives in an environment rich with stimulating things to do will be far less likely to exhibit aggression towards people. Remember when using toys to vary them daily so your cat doesn't get bored. He will enjoy himself much more if you rotate them.

2: Don't use your hands and feet to tease and play with your cat. This will just tell him that biting and scratching a person is acceptable. Always use a toy. A piece of string or a sock.

3: Minor punishment in the event of aggressive behaviour is acceptable and I wouldn't feel bad about using. Things such as squirting him with water, making a sudden noise such as by dropping some keys or firmly saying but not shouting 'No' will discourage him from said behaviour.

Under no circumstances should you hit or severely discipline a playful cat so if you have children then please make them mindful of this. Doing this won't help and will usually worsen the aggression problem. Punishment alone won't work, what will work is encouraging appropriate play and implementing the minor deterrents I mention above.

Petting aggression: You might be familiar with petting your cat and then he suddenly bites or scratches you. This is common behaviour but it's not well understood even by esteemed animal behaviourists. Whatever your cat's motive, one minute you're enjoying bonding together and the next the situation becomes unpleasant. What we do know is that biting or scratching means he's had enough and he wants you to stop immediately. Different cats vary in how much petting they will tolerate before they lash out, and some cats simply never do it. As with all aggressive behaviour males have more of a predisposition to demonstrate it, but even the most relaxed and chilled out female might exhibit it now and again.

Many people think that this aggression comes out of the blue and there is nothing they can do to forecast it but this is a misnomer and you can look for certain signals and patterns of body language which will suggest lashing out is imminent. Signs that this might happen are increasing restlessness in your cat. His tail may become to twitch and he might start licking his lips. His ears might go back or flick back and forth and he might start turning his head and looking at your hand with a vested interest!

Obviously as soon as you detect such behaviour you should stop petting your cat if you want to avoid being bitten or scratched. Just leave him alone and give him some space, don't tease or taunt him and remember to never hit your pet because this will just make it worse and make him associate petting with being punished, thusly damaging your relationship.

You can manipulate your cat into tolerating longer periods of petting by using trusty food rewards. When you first detect signs that your cat might lash out then give him a nice treat. The idea behind this is that he will associate being petted with being given treats and will hopefully start to tolerate longer sessions. Just remember to always stop the petting when you identify any of the aggressive signs I mentioned to avoid being attacked!

Other kinds of aggression: Some cats get aggressive for reasons unknown to us, we must remember that even domesticated cats are still animals and thusly their behaviour can never be completely predictable. Remember to never try and handle an aggressive or fearful cat, if you do this then it could lash out. Fortunately in my experience none of my cats have displayed pathological levels of aggression but if your pet ever does then you must contact a vet for a check up. Certain illnesses, ailments and conditions can result in feline aggression so this shows the issue isn't always a behavioural problem.

AGGRESSION TOWARDS OTHER CATS

Cats are naturally quite solitary creatures and do not live within large social networks that say dogs do. Sometimes cats can get along just fine but tensions can start to rise if several cats for example share the same small living space.

As I touched on in the socialisation section, the better a cat is socialised in kitten hood with other kittens, the more likely it will be sociable and friendly with other cats as an adult. However if you adopt a stray street-cat then it's likely this kind of feline will not be well socialised with other cats and this could result in inter-cat fighting if you have a multi-cat home. Cats tend to fight for the following reasons.

1: As we know, cats are territorial so territorial aggression happens when another cat encroaches on his home. Males and females are equally territorial about their living spaces and can result in hissing and spitting at the other feline and can eventually manifest into fighting. This can happen when a new tenant arrives but don't worry I will explain how to avoid these circumstances below.

2: Defensive aggression can happen when a cat attacks another to protect himself from a perceived threat he cannot avoid.

3: Redirected aggression is quite a strange concept. Say your cats inside and he sees a bird outside through the window. Because he doesn't have access to the bird through the glass he might instead lash out at another cat inside acting as a conduit for his aggression. To the untrained eye it would look like a pointless, arbitrary attack but it's born out of frustration at not being able to have access to that tasty looking bird outside.

The first thing you need to do if you witness your cats inter-feline fighting is to stop it as soon as possible before anyone can get hurt. Whatever you do don't pull them apart or drag them away from each other; instead make a loud noise or squirt them with water, even throw a soft toy at them. Consider keeping the aggressors away from each other and if you detect any aggressive behaviour brewing then intervene before it's too late. Do not attempt to punish any suchlike behaviour by hitting or slapping your cats, this will not work and could make the problem worse than it already is.

You should also work on modifying your cat's behaviour to avoid any aggression. This is not as complicated or difficult as it sounds and involves teaching your pet to respond to another cat in a non aggressive manner. Surprise, surprise you may not be totally shocked to learn that again you can manipulate your cats to behave better with the promise of a food treat. Next time they are together reward them with a treat so your cats are programmed to associate pleasant things (food) with behaving well in each other's presence. If you do this you'll be surprised how quickly the cats begin to tolerate each other.

The reality is that different cats will always respond differently to other felines and it's not an exact science. Many aggression problems can be solved if you follow the above steps but if they do persist then please contact your vet or an animal behavioural specialist. They might provide you with special cat medications that make cats more placid and likely to get on with each other. Do not give your pet any human medication; these can be toxic to cats.

Don't forget that it might take time but most inter-cat problems can be reduced to practically nothing. Although they might not be best mates, they will at least extend the courtesy of tolerating each other.

CAT HEALTH PROBLEMS

To help you fully care for your cat I think it's necessary to include a section on potential health concerns. There are simple steps you can take to make sure your cat stays strong and lives a healthy and very happy life with you. Sadly even the best kept cats can be susceptible to certain sicknesses and illnesses. Without meaning to worry you I will make you aware of the symptoms and warning signs of various cat health issues that will help you know what to do should they ever arise.

THE MOUTH AND TEETH

The mouth and teeth are prone to various problems

Mouth inflammation or infection: Caused by bones stuck between the teeth or gums and viral infections, poor oral care, and kidney failure causing painful stomatitis.

This can be treated at the vets. They will remove all foreign objects from the mouth such as fish bones. Dental problems are resolved and the vet will provide you with antibiotics for your cat which will cure any ensuing bacterial infection.

Mouth tumours: Many older cats get mouth tumours. If you identify an unusual swelling on the roof of your cat's mouth, tongue or in the jaw coupled with bad breath then please take him to the vet.

Gum disease: Most cats develop gum disease at some point in their lives, a product of poor dental hygiene and viral infections. The main symptom will be bad breath. Gum disease in older cats may also be a result of Kidney failure.

This can be treated in the same way that human gum disease is, by the vet scaling and polishing the teeth and removing plaque and tartar.

Tooth-root abscess: Upper premolars are most prone to an abscess. This may be identified firstly by a swelling below your cat's eye. Eventually the abscess will break through his skin.

The vet will remove the teeth to avoid any further complications.

Don't forget the best way to maintain healthy cat teeth and gums is by letting them have a good old chew and gnaw. Small fish bones are a good idea and most cats are intelligent to chew them thoroughly before swallowing!

THE EARS

Wounds: If your cat's been in a fight his ear flaps might be wounded and therefore it's likely there will be an infection.

As soon as you notice a wound then take your cat to the vet who will give you antibiotics to treat the infection.

Haematoma: This is a large blood blister within the ear flap caused by excessive scratching or fighting with another cat.

This will be easily identifiable because the swollen ear flap will be blatant and your cat may even tilt his head to the affected side and shake it.

Your vet will be able to treat this condition by performing an operation to remove the blood and preserve the shape of the ear. The success rate is high but don't forget if the scratching is caused by parasites for example then that will also need to be treated.

The best thing to do to help maintain clean ears and avoid infections is to routinely clean them with a small amount of olive oil or baby oil on a soft cotton wool ball. Do not use a cotton wool stick.

THE EYES

Third eyelid: This is the strange occurrence of a third eyelid partially covering an otherwise healthy eye. This is not a sign of blindness in your pet so don't worry but is sometimes an early symptom of cat influenza. The condition is characterised by the protrusion of a white skin over some of the eye (s) from the inner corner.

Fortunately in the modern age there are treatments for this condition. Your vet may numb the eye with anaesthetic drops and remove any foreign objects that may be trapped. He may also be able to use surgical instruments to detect infecting bacteria and use further surgery to correct other eye problems including cataracts and blocked tear ducts.

Inflammation and soreness: If your cat's eyes are inflamed and sore then he's been wounded or has an infection and will require immediate treatment. Symptoms will be red and sore looking eyes which are seeping discharge.

If your pet doesn't seem in any considerable discomfort then feel free to deposit some Golden Eye Liquid (Available online and in most pharmacies worldwide) into the eye. If the condition is causing your cat distress then you must take him to the vet. The vet will be able to provide you with some more cat-orientated eye drops if the Golden Eye Liquid hasn't improved things. If the inflammation and soreness is a result of foreign bodies trapped in your cat's eye then he may require minor surgery to remove it.

PARASITES

Fleas and mites: Cats can easily become infected with fleas. You'll be able to see them and their droppings amongst your pet's hair. These will cause itching which may result in damaging the skin and fleas also carry certain diseases and carry tapeworm larvae. Orange specks in your cats fur is a sign of harvest mites, most common in the summertime.

The best way to treat fleas and mites is by investing in some anti-parasitic powder or aerosol. Make sure you get a product that contains methoprene and permethrin because this destroys the flea eggs and prevents any future egg hatching. You could also consider visiting the vet for some hardcore parasite ass kicking treatment such as special injections and drops. Don't worry, fleas and mites infecting cats is very common but very easy to treat.

Ringworm: These can cause skin disease and are characterised by resulting in powdery and scaly skin or even bald circular areas.

Again this can easily be treated by drugs that your vet will be able to give you

INTERNAL PARASITES

Roundworms: These blighters reside in the cat's intestinal canal and are round as their name suggests and can be up to four inches long. They resemble spaghetti and absorb all the nutrients up from his food. Symptoms of having roundworm include when your cat's coat is noticeably more dull than usual, he has a pot-bellied appearance and he may vomit them up or you might notice them in his faeces.

Treatment is straightforward and normally successful. Your vet will give you the medication required to get rid of them and you might consider regular deworming treatment to make sure they don't return.

Tapeworms: These are another common parasite which is picked up when a cat eats an infected flea. As the disgusting creature is digested within the cat's intestine, the tapeworm is released and it hatches and attaches to the intestinal lining. You might see these in your cat's anus.

The vet will be able to provide your cat with an injection or tablets that will swiftly deal with the infection. Side effects are very rare and at the worst include short-term diarrhoea and vomiting.

Whipworms: Cats transmit these lovely fellows through ingestion of infested matter. Whipworm eggs can be present in soil, food, and water, as well as in faeces and animal flesh. They can also be contracted from other animals. Whipworms can affect cats of all ages. Symptoms of this condition include bloody diarreah, dehydration, anaemia and weight loss.

If you suspect your cat has whipworm then as you probably expect your vet will be able to prescribe suitable medication that will kill the worms and the larvae living within his body. To prevent your pet being infected again avoid putting your cat in close quarters with other animals for long period and make sure his living area is always clean.

Toxoplasmosis: These are single celled organisms that unfortunately are able to sexually reproduce within cats. Most cats don't show symptoms of being infected by this ghastly parasite but those that do show signs of lethargy, fever and loss of appetite. Your cat will most likely pick up this condition from eating already infected prey such as rodents.

Treatment will be with medication prescribed by your vet such as Pyrimethamine, Clindamycin and Sulfadiazine.

STOMACH PROBLEMS

Vomiting: Vomiting is usually transient and will go away by itself. The most common causes of this are Gastritis which is a mild inflammation of the stomach caused by the ingestion of certain chemicals, and fur balls which build up within your cat and are eventually thrown up.

If your cat has been vomiting then don't feed him any solid food for a few hours and if it continues then try and give him a tasty liquid replacement such as chicken soup.

In more rare situations excessive and continued vomiting could be a symptom of an infection, intestinal obstruction or tumour so if it persists for longer than a day I'd suggest medical attention.

Diarrhoea: This could be the result of a mild bowel infection or too much liver to eat so generally it isn't too serious.

If it become excessive and lasts longer than just a usual bout then it could be a sign of an infection so please consult your vet.

Overeating: This is normal behaviour if a cat is convalescing after an illness or she's just given birth.

If it persists then it could be a sign of parasites, diabetes or even hormonal disease so take your cat to the vet.

Excessive thirst: If your cat starts to drink excessively and this is becoming a worry then it could be that he has diabetes, liver or kidney problems.

Take him to the vets if you notice he's drinking loads more than usual but don't forget like humans, cats need to hydrate more in warm weather.

Blood in stools: This could be a result of food-poisoning or maybe something innocent like bits of bone scratching the intestinal lining.

If bloody stools persist then it's time for a trip to Mr Vet.

Lack of appetite: This can occur for many reasons ranging from non-serious to serious.

If your cats eating patterns show a big change over the space of more than a few days then consider medical help.

RESPIRATORY PROBLEMS

A cat's nose, throat and sinuses are prone to infections caused by various bacteria and viruses. They are prevalent in shelters, catteries and multi-cat households and are usually transmitted from cat to cat by sneezing, coughing, sharing food and water and grooming each other. Chlamydia is a typical bacterial infection commonly found in shelters and places were cats live in close proximity.

Symptoms of respiratory problems will differ but will generally be characterised by your cat coughing and sneezing, gasping for air and a very laboured type of breathing.

The best ways of ensuring your cat doesn't get affected are by.

1: Making sure he is up to date with his vaccines.

2: Practicing good hygiene and washing your hands properly when handling multiple cats.

3: Ensure your cat has frequent veterinary examinations so that any problems can be detected early and preventative measures can be employed before anything serious develops.

If your cat is unfortunate enough to be afflicted with a respiratory condition then your vet will be able to prescribe special medicines and antibiotics. If you get your pet vaccinated as a kitten against the likes of Chlamydia and Feline influenza then it should prevent any severe disease spreading.

URINARY DISORDERS

Kidney disease: This is common especially amongst older cats and is characterised by an increased amount of drinking, blood in the urine and weight loss. Other symptoms are vomiting, bad breath and anaemia.

If you suspect your cat might be affected then please go and visit your vet. He will help you devise a special kidney diet for your cat which will help support the remaining functioning kidney tissue.

Blood in the urine: This may indicate a bladder infection, bladder or kidney stones or poisoning from certain chemicals found in rodenticide.

If you notice this then you must see your vet the same day if possible.

Thirst and weight loss: These can both be due to kidney disease as I explained, but they also are a result of other diseases such as diabetes.

To help prevent this you must make sure your cat has plenty of fresh water available and moist, fresh food.

Further urinary problems: Frequent urination and reoccurring cystitis are mainly symptomatic of older cats and can explain why accidents can occur to felines despite being fully toilet-trained.

Never punish or discipline your cat for any toilet 'accidents' because it will just upset and stress him out. Instead you must consult your vet who will be able to help the situation.

NUTRITIONAL PROBLEMS

Vitamin deficiency: A diet of exclusively meat can result in a vitamin A or D deficiency. Indications of vitamin A deficiency are bone, skin and eye disease as well as general poor condition and even infertility. Signs of vitamin D deficiency are bone disease but fortunately this can be arrested with a more balanced diet and cod liver oil supplements.

Most commercial cat foods contain vitamin B. If you feed your cat too much raw meat and fish then it may have a vitamin B deficiency which can result in a stroke or convulsion. Too much over-processed food can lead to an anaemia, weight loss and convulsions as well.

Vitamin B deficiencies can easily be treated with Vitamin B injections, yeast and B-complex tablets, oral supplements and by improving your cat's diet

Mineral deficiency: If your cat doesn't get enough calcium in his diet then he may develop rickets, especially if he's young; if he's older then brittle bones may occur.

Making sure your pet gets plenty of milk, fish and good quality commercial foods will prevent any of the above happening. You could also lightly season your cat's food with iodized salt to make sure he gets the iodine he needs in his diet, or mix in multi-vitamin trace element tablets especially made for small animals.

Obesity: It's remarkable how many cat owners over feed and under-administer their cats exercise regimes. A cat shouldn't weigh more than 8kg and if he does he's obese and you need to put him on a diet and get him fit before the extra weight puts strain on his heart and liver. In my opinion letting your cat get to the stage of obesity is disgusting and akin to animal abuse.

Too much fat in the diet will obviously cause obesity such as fatty fish as well as general over-indulgence. You can manage obesity yourself prescribing the right diet for your cat and your vet may help providing you with large doses of vitamin E supplements if he gets too big.

REPRODUCTIVE PROBLEMS

Infertility: A common reason that a Queen doesn't become pregnant is poor breeding management. She needs to allow a male to mate with her before she will ovulate. 3-4 breedings a day every 1-2 days is ideal. If two cats take a disliking to each other and refuse to mate then consider finding another partner.

Underweight and overweight Queens also have more problems conceiving and feeding your cat low quality food may also affect pregnancy. Other reasons may be an infection of the uterus, vagina or pyometra.

If you have a problem then reproductive specialists are readily available at many veterinary teaching hospitals and they will be able to assist.

Miscarriage: it's not uncommon for cats to have spontaneous abortions (miscarriages) You can identify if your cat has had one by abnormal vaginal bleeding and an extended amount of vaginal discharge. If she was in the late trimester then you may even find an expelled foetus.

Cats that experience a spontaneous abortion should be taken to the vet immediately where the condition will be diagnosed and a variety of medical treatment options will be considered.

Mastitis: This is an inflammation and infection of the mammary glands. Symptoms will include warm, painful or hard mammary glands and milk will be off-colour and clumping. Your cat may also have a fever.

This can be treated by your vet with antibiotics, hot packing the affected glands and milking out the affected glands. If the milk remains normal then it's safe for the kittens to nurse from the affected glands.

Metritis: Another inflammation and infection which this time occurs in the uterus. Symptoms will be quite obvious and include an off-colour bad smelling vaginal discharge. Loss of appetite, depression, thirst, vomiting, fever and general restlessness.

If you detect this than urgent veterinary attention is required and treatment will involve antibiotics, fluids and sometimes spay surgery.

Pyometra: An infection of the uterus that occurs after heat cycles where the Queen doesn't become pregnant. Symptoms may include vomiting, lack of appetite and an increased thirst. If your cat's cervix is open then a vaginal discharge may be seen, if the cervix is closed then no discharge will be seen.

Your vet will usually administer a hysterectomy, or the removal of the diseased womb through an incision under general anaesthetic.

Lack of maternal instinct: Some cats can have a lack of natural maternal instinct due to environmental disturbances. It is also sometimes a result of genetic or illness. Some first time Queens will take a while to understand their role as a mother and will sometimes need a helping hand in the right direction from you.

After the delivery you may notice small temperamental changes in your cat. If this is a problem then that line of cats shouldn't be used for breeding anymore. Sometimes cannibalism of kittens can occur in inexperienced Queens or older ones. If you're breeding and you notice this trait then again you must remove this cat and her relatives from the breeding programme.

Avoiding unwanted pregnancies: Castrating Toms and spaying Queens is the only way you can avoid unwanted pregnancies. These operations will also make Toms stray less, fight less and stop them from spraying territory with urine markers. It also means the Queens won't be bothered as much by the neighbourhood Romeos and the community isn't constantly disturbed by the howling of a female on heat.

If you want your Queen to breed but with control and without the problems associated with a female on heat then the oestrus (heat) can be suppressed using tablets and injections that your vet will be able to inform you about. These drugs will allow a return to the normal sexual cycle when you want her to have kittens. You could also consider asking the vet about the female contraceptive pill but I must advise that these do cause side effects such as weight gain and increased appetite.

Castration: Toms can be castrated once they're six months old but just to be safe I'd advise waiting until at least 9 months to avoid the possibility of urinary blockages in the penis in later life.

Spaying: Females should be spayed ideally when they're between four and nine months old. Under no circumstances should a kitten under the age of three months ever be spayed.

BLOOD AND CIRCULATION PROBLEMS

Heart problems: Unfortunately cats are susceptible to several heart conditions, kittens can be born with congenital defects. They are also prone to viruses and bacterial diseases which can cause long-term heart tissue damage. The heart can also develop tumours and heart valves can become blocked, especially in older cats. Over-active thyroid glands can also affect the feline heart.

Common symptoms may be faster than usual or laboured breathing patterns, coughing, wheezing and tiring quickly. If one of these conditions last for longer than two days then please consult your vet.

The vet will use X-rays, electrocardiography, ultra-sound or blood analysis to help diagnose the issue. Weak hearts can be treated with certain drugs and tiring hearts can be strengthened with vitamin E supplements. Please ask your vet for a more definitive list of treatments.

Anaemia: Anaemia is a deficiency of red blood cells circulating in the blood. Typical symptoms are invariably breathlessness, fatigue, restlessness and also pale mouth and eye membranes.

This may come about for three main reasons.

1: Red blood cells are destroyed by parasites, bacterial toxins and poisons.

2: Blood is lost from chronic bleeding, wounds, ulcers, internal tumours, blood sucking parasites and ingestion of certain chemicals.

3: Red blood cells in the bone marrow are reduced because of acute and chronic infections, poisons, tumours, kidney disease and diets bereft of some essential elements.

The affliction will be treated by your vet and may include a course of vitamins, iron supplements and even a potential blood transfusion.

Feline infectious anaemia: This is caused by parasites which live inside the cat's red blood cells. In small numbers they won't cause any ill-effects but in large numbers they're dangerous and can destroy the cells.

The usual symptoms will be weight loss, loss of appetite, fever, depression, general weakness and lethargy.

It can be treated with certain antibiotics, anti-anaemic therapy and in some cases a blood transfusion.

Thrombosis: The blocking of a vein or artery by a clot in the bloodstream can be fatal.

General symptoms are very bleak and include sudden collapse, pain and even paralysis of the hind legs.

If you detect this condition in your cat then you must seek medical attention as soon as possible. Sadly recovery rate is low but the quicker you see a vet the better chance your pet has.

Feline leukaemia: This is a retrovirus that can severely inhibit a cat's immune system. It's one of the most common diseases and causes of death amongst domestic cats. Luckily some cats are naturally immune but others carry and transmit it to other felines sometimes without ever showing signs of illness. If you are breeding cats or live in a multi-cat household then I'm afraid you will have to isolate the afflicted cat.

Common symptoms are loss of appetite and weight loss, abscesses, poor coat condition, pale or inflamed gums, diarrhoea and vomiting, eye problems, enlarged lymph nodes, female reproductive problems, jaundice, chronic skin disease, lethargy and respiratory problems. In some cases as I mentioned above the condition is entirely asymptomatic.

I'm afraid to say there is no cure to feline leukaemia and unfortunately euthanising the cat may be the only way to avoid transmitting it to other felines. Cats that develop this condition can be treated with chemotherapy but this only focuses on prolonging life a little bit and providing him with the best quality of life possible.

MUSCLE, BONE AND JOINT PROBLEMS

Arthritis: This happens when the joint cartilage is unable to maintain a healthy state or repair normally after damage.

If your cat has arthritis then you will notice certain things such as stiffness, limping, muscle atrophy, difficulty getting up after lying down and restricted jumping and climbing ability.

Degenerative joint disease can be treated surgically and medically. Reducing inflammation and pain is key to providing a good quality of life for your cat. Your vet will recommend which anti-inflammatory drug to give your pet. Never try and give your cat human medication such as aspirin because these are unsafe for cats to take.

Lameness: Bone, muscle and joint disorders are usually painful which results in lameness. Lameness might be spinal cord damage, limping, bone tumours, ligament tears, sprains, strains and cut pads amongst other things.

Treatments will vary depending on the type of lameness but rest assured that most conditions can be corrected with surgery or cured with medications. The feline body is very strong and resilient and in most cases your cat should overcome the problem.

Joint injuries: joint injuries and dislocations are usually a result of physical trauma.

Dislocated bones can thankfully be manually replaced under a local anaesthetic.

Broken bones: An open fracture will be obvious. With a closed fracture the break isn't visible but can cause great pain and swelling.

Try not to touch the site of the break and use a clean towel to clean wounds if there are any. Once your cat has recovered from the shock of the trauma then get him to a vet as soon as you can.

Muscles: Tearing, bruising and strains are common complaints that can affect your cat. They are usually caused by physical trauma such as falls and fighting.

Symptoms such as reddening caused by muscle damage will be revealed if you part the hair between your fingers.

The best treatment is just rest and relaxation which I'm sure your cat will have had lots of practice at. You could also consider cold packs to help swelling and tenderness.

NERVOUS SYSTEM PROBLEMS

Encephalitis: This is an inflammation of the brain caused by bacteria, poisons, viruses or parasites via the blood or nearby tissues.

Symptoms can be fever, staggering, weakness, paralysis, coma, dilated pupils and epileptic fits.

If your cat shows any of these symptoms then you must see the vet straight away. Treatment will involve antibiotics and corticosteroids.

Epileptic fits: These will happen quickly and seemingly randomly and the cat will fall over and start shuddering, usually foaming at the mouth. After a few minutes the episode usually stops and your cat will regain his bearings and stand up again as if nothing happened. This may be caused by parasites, head injuries or even tumours but don't worry too much because your cat won't have suffered any pain.

The best thing to do if your cat breaks out into a fit is to darken the room if possible and reduce all ambient noise e.g. turn the radio off. Don't attempt to touch the cat or intervene and make sure you take him to see the vet when he's recovered.

Myelitis: This condition is the inflammation of the spinal cord and is usually caused by a bacterial infection in nearby tissues. Most cases originate from deep cat bites to the back which may happen during fights, but also from parasites, poisons and certain viruses.

The symptoms will be fairly obvious and will include partial or total paralysis of one or more limbs.

If you suspect your cat has been afflicted with myelitis then he will require fast medical attention. Remember to move him very gently when taking him to the vets to prevent any unnecessary pain.

Treatment will feature draining the spinal canal and by prescribing drugs. If your cat is paralysed then sadly the outlook isn't good if he doesn't improve much in a month and full recovery may take several months. Physiotherapy will also help recovery but this may be time consuming and expensive.

Local nerve paralysis: Part of your cat's body might become paralysed if a nerve suddenly stops working properly. This is most likely to happen with the tail or a limb because of a physical trauma. Your pet won't be able to feel or control the affected body part and so he will drag it around across the ground which will result in abrasions and eventually ulceration.

If this happens to your cat then please seek medical attention as soon as possible. If treatment doesn't trigger an improvement in a month or so then sadly amputation of the affected appendage will be required.

SKIN AND COAT PROBLEMS

Unfortunately skin and coat problems are quite common and in fact account for up to fifty percent of all trips to the vets in the UK and USA. Parasites such as fleas and mites are often culpable but there are sometimes other explanations.

To make a diagnosis your vet might examine your pet's skin with an ultraviolet light looking for ringworm, he may take a scrape for parasites, a smear for bacteria or even a biopsy which can reveal cellular changes. Blood and skin tests, diet and environmental changes can also be used to diagnose skin disorders.

Signs of skin disease: This can be identified by excessive scratching resulting in hair loss, pigment changes, visible lumps, inflammation, dry scales and ulcers. Usually skin disease will be indicated by more than one of these signs.

Itchy skin: If your cat starts to excessively scratch then it could be parasites, as I mentioned above fleas and mites but also potentially maggots, lice and in hot climes mosquitoes. Allergies are also a common cause of scratching and this can also be coupled with excessive licking and grooming.

Pimples, crusting skin and scaling: Pus filled pimples called pustules are a common skin complaint. You will easily be able to feel them through your cat's hair and when they eventually burst they lead to skin erosion. Allergies such as flea-allergy dermatitis, food-allergy dermatitis, contact-allergy dermatitis and military eczema are the most common reason for these pustules.

Crusting skin is a consequence of skin damage and scaling of the skin is when bits flake off and resemble particles of dandruff.

If your cat develops any of these skin conditions then seek medical assistance.

Cat bite wounds: Skin swelling around the face, neck and tail is a sign your cat has been in the wars. Cat bite abscesses will require surgical draining, cleansing and a course of antibiotics.

Hair loss: Unlike humans hair loss is usually limited to partial or local. It can occur when new hair fails to grow, is licked out, scratched out or just spontaneously falls out. It can also be caused by: parasitic and fungal infection, environmental and behavioural reasons, excessive grooming, drug reaction, overactive adrenal gland and burns.

Skin lumps: These include cysts, abscess, lipoma, melanoma, histiocytoma and warts. Ask your vet immediately for a more in depth description of these conditions and treatment if you discover your cat does have lumps or bumps.

Swollen pads: If you notice swollen pads which also cause lameness then your vet will be able to prescribe suitable medication for your pet.

Mouth ulcer: If your cat has a lip ulcer or one on the chin then the condition can be dealt simply with medication so go see the vet.

CAT INSURANCE, DO YOU NEED IT?

There are various things you should consider when considering cat insurance. Admittedly the concept of pet insurance might be as necessary as life insurance for humans to some people but in reality only the minority of owners actually insure their cats. I personally haven't done it and thank the Lord none of my cats has ever had a serious affliction that a quick check-up at the vets couldn't deal with.

If you have the money to spare and you can comfortably afford it then you should go ahead; but I see it as a bit of a gamble. You're betting your cat will need it at some stage in his life and you're paying a premium for that right every month. I'm going to go on to a few things you will need to know when thinking about a policy.

Some insurance companies stipulate that you have to use a vet that is registered on their approved list. If your usual vet wasn't on the list then you would have to see someone else and who's to say where the closest one to your house is based? Always ask if you have a free choice of veterinarian before you sign the line which is dotted.

All cat policies have exclusions unfortunately. A common one is the pre-existing condition exclusion which is loosely defined as injuries and medical conditions that were evident prior to signing up.

Other exclusions I have heard about are neutering and spaying, vaccinations, flea control, dental care and heartworm medication. Pay very close attention to the policy and its exclusions. Unfairly or not some people enrol without doing the necessary homework and just assume common feline problems such as flea control are included. When they find out they are wrong it can be very distressing and you have to spend extra cash to get your cat treated as well as being stuck with paying for the existing policy!

Many companies also charge an excess or flat deductible fee, depending on your cat's age for every single treatment. This means regardless of the procedure you have to pay them an amount of money upfront which can be as high as $100 (£64) as well as contributing up to 20% of the vet's fee AS WELL as your monthly policy fee. Companies do this to reduce the number of total claims against them and to stop time-wasters and unnecessary procedures.

Another thing you should consider is that many companies operate a maximum claim policy. This would mean that they only would pay out a certain amount for a given illness, regardless if your cat was better or not. Some companies have annual caps which cannot be exceeded that year and also lifetime caps.

In the end it's entirely up to you, insurance can give you peace of mind but I always think paying for veterinary costs as you go is cheaper than paying monthly for a policy. Having said that, you don't know what the future holds and if your cat gets unwell then you will be relieved you did enrol in the first place. If you do decide to then I must reiterate that you check and double check the policy for exclusions. Have a look at that small print and only sign for it when you're absolutely sure it's the right thing for you and your cat.

CARING FOR THE ELDERLY CAT

Cats are living longer and longer than ever now due to advances in medical care and improved nutritional knowledge. In the cat world felines aged over ten are considered 'seniors' or 'old aged pensioners' and those aged fifteen and above are thought to be 'geriatric'.

Unfortunately growing old is one of life's inalienable truths for cats as well as people. As a cat approaches the winter of his life you will notice various changes in his physicality and general behaviour.

1: Older cats become less active and his muscle tone will reduce which will affect his ability to climb, run and jump as he used to do. Lack of exercise will make this worse, so if you have an elderly cat don't allow him to be too lazy because this will contribute to the stiffening of joints.

2: His vision and hearing will get worse and you may find he's easily startled.

3: His appetite will decrease and the senses of smell and taste will deteriorate. He may also be more likely to develop teeth and gum problems.

4: Bowel function may get worse as well. Your cat might struggle to absorb food nutrients which can result in weight loss. Some older cats also suffer from constipation.

5: He will tend to sleep for even longer and at more regular intervals.

6: The immune system will become less efficient with age resulting in increased propensity of developing infections

When your cat approaches ten years old you should remember to get him checked out regularly by the vet. Many surgeries even have clinics designed exclusively for the older cat! A thorough examination will be conducted checking for the various health problems your pet may be susceptible to.

Frequent booster vaccinations should also be considered. It is widely thought that the immune system deteriorates with age, resulting in an increased vulnerability to certain infections. Boosters help stimulate the immune system and help your cat defeat these infections.

As cats get older they may develop weight problems. Some become fat after the age of ten but usually by the teenage years they become thin. Regular weighing is therefore important.

Feeding tips: Elderly cats require more water than their youthful counterparts so a tinned food diet with high water content is most suitable. Your pet should also have lots of fresh water readily available. You should strongly consider integrating dry food into your cat's diet if you don't already because this can assist in reducing the build up of tartar on the teeth.

Making your cat comfortable: I always think it's nice to extend a little extra attention to an older cat. Elderly felines should have a comfortable, warm bed in a draught free part of the house where they can sleep soundly without disturbances. They also tend to like to stretch out so consider investing in a bean bag or a hammock bed that you can station on a radiator, all of these things will be greatly appreciated!

Extra attention should also be paid to an older cat's nails. These are harder to retract and can get trapped easier in the carpet and other surfaces. If they're overgrown they can potentially stick into the pads too! An elderly cat will also need to be groomed more frequently because he'll be less able to do it himself. Make sure you look out for any lumps on the skin or any fleas in the hair.

Please also bear in mind that if you have children, dogs or other younger more playful cats then the older cat should be given his space away from these. As a young animal he could hold his own but most older cats like to enjoy a rest away from the noise and excitement.

You should also consider providing indoor litter trays as bladder control and bowel movements tend to become more unpredictable. Use large, shallow trays for easy access and buy a soft litter such as sand based one which will be more comfortable to stand on.

Health problems in older cats: I touched on many of these in the health problems section but elderly cats are more susceptible to afflictions such as kidney failure, overactive thyroid gland, sugar diabetes, high blood pressure, cancer, periodontal disease and arthritis.

Sadly older cats can have several of these problems concurrently so taking him to the vet as soon as you suspect something is wrong is of paramount importance.

Medication for the older cat: Kidney and liver disease can affect an elderly cat's ability to cope with certain medication. Many drugs are broken down and eliminated from the body by the kidneys and liver so diseases of these organs can mean build up of drugs in the bloodstream which can potentially reach toxic levels. Your vet will be able to advise you more extensively if you have any concerns.

You must remember that for an older cat medical treatment is more of a management technique than an actual cure. Treatments should be stopped if they're causing unacceptable side effects or are severely distressing or upsetting your pet. Quality of life for an older cat is the most important thing.

Cats age a lot faster than humans do as you can see below

Cat years	Human years	Cat years	Human years
1	15	11	60
2	24	12	64
3	28	13	68
4	32	14	72
5	36	15	76
6	40	16	80
7	44	17	84
8	48	18	88
9	52	19	92
10	56	20	96

BEREAVEMENT

I've bred and owned cats for many years and it's also extremely sad when you see your long time friend and companion pass away. The ancient Egyptian's mourned the death of cats with equal intensity as if they lost a human relative and would shave their eyebrows as a sign of the loss. Different people react to death in different ways from my experiences.

Reasons for death: There are two main reasons for this.

1: Death through physical trauma or illness.

2: Euthanasia (Putting your cat to sleep when the alternative would be to live with severe mental or physical trauma causing a poor quality of life)

Euthanasia: Bringing your pet to peace in the most dignified and humane way is most important. It is quick and less painful than a slow, natural death at the hands of an accident or illness. Your vet can arrange to come to your house to put your cat down or you can go to the clinic.

At your house: You can help to keep your cat calm to make the process as easy and stress free as possible. Keep his routine as normal so you don't upset him and make sure you separate having given him lots of love and attention.

At the vets: I'd advise having a friend or family member take you as support, I know I never feel like driving home after. Make sure you bring a blanket if you want to bring him home again after for burial.

The process: Thankfully the process is fast and painless. If your pet's extremely distressed then a sedative will be used. The vet will shave his foreleg to locate the vein and then a concentrated barbiturate (anaesthetic overdose) will be administered into that vein. He will instantaneously fall asleep and moments later he will stop breathing and his heart will stop. If the vein on the foreleg is not easy to find, which may happen to a cat with circulatory system problems then the injection will be administered into the chest or abdomen.

Afterwards: Pet cemeteries and crematoriums will tell you what it costs and what the process involves. You may decide to take your pet home and bury him yourself. The grave should be at least 1m deep to stop animals from digging it up.

Grieving process: As I said, different people respond differently to the death of a beloved pet. Grieving is a natural and central part of the healing process and only time will tell you how long this will be for.

If you need support you can always turn to close friends and family member for emotional support and there are many pet-bereavement services you can consider which can easily be found on Google. You could also consider going to see a doctor or a bereavement counsellor if you need to.

I think it's a good idea and helps the healing process if you mark your pet's grave in some way, such as with a headstone, plant or tree. You then have something palpable to remember him by.

Children and pet loss: For many children losing a pet might be the first time in their life they experience loss. Don't tell them that he's been put to sleep and just remember to be as supportive and understanding as possible. You could also consider a child counsellor if you think that would help.

Time for a new cat? : Eventually you may feel like you would like a new cat. There is no shame or dishonour in this. There are thousands of lovely cats in rescue shelters and in charities that would absolutely love to come and live with you. You will never forget your cat but there's something special in offering a new cat the love, care and attention that he deserves.

A PHYSICAL OVERVIEW OF CATS

There are around 100 different breeds of cat in the world and they all have a similar body structure. Their bodies, sensory organs and natural instincts are perfectly designed for them to hunt and survive out in the wild.

Cats usually weight between 2.5 and 7kg (5.5-16 pounds) although some breeds are known to weigh more than 11kg (25 pounds) Overfeeding can result in obesity and a weight of up to 23kg (50 pounds) This is rare though and equally unhealthy and potentially fatal. Obesity can be controlled with a good diet and regular exercise.

Body: The average cat measures around 30 inches (76.2 cm) from nose to tail and has around 244 bones. They have 30 vertebrae in their spinal column which accounts for their amazing flexibility and agility. This also allows a cat to jump around five times its own body height, climb up trees and chase after prey.

Ears: Cats are deaf at birth; their hearing begins to develop at approximately two weeks. Thirty-two muscles in each ear enable directional hearing, this means that a cat can move its ears independently of each other and in opposite directions to the way the body is facing. This is an essential tool in the wild to help them hunt and alert them of potential dangers. Cats have straight ears that point upwards. When a cat is angry or frightened his ears may turn back but this also happens when he's carefully listening to a sound. The position of the cat's ear can help you understand his mood.

Cats can hear much higher pitched sounds than humans and even dogs. From a distance of three feet they can differentiate between sources of sound as little as three inches apart!

The inner ear is responsible for amazing feline balancing ability. The tiny chamber and ear canals are lined with millions of sensitive hairs that contain fluid and floating crystals. When a cat changes position, these hairs detect movement of the fluid and crystals and send immediate signals to the brain. These signals give the brain pin-point readings on the body position allowing the muscles to compensate and help maintain a perfect balance. This also explains why in most cases a cat will land on his feet!

Eyes: Even domestic cats are predators and will have some hunting ability. Cat's eyesight enables them to be deadly, efficient hunters. The eyes are located on the front of the head which provides them with superior depth perception compared to a creature that's eyes are on the side of the head.

Depth perception is vital when considering hunting because the cat will need to know how far he has to pounce to catch his prey. It will also enable him to judge the distances of jumps when he's playing in the house leaping across the room.

Cats are active at both day and night but their special eyesight provides them with exceptional abilities in poor lightening. In low-light it is said that cats can see around six times better than humans!

Cat's pupils can be round when dilated, or can shrink in from the sides until its elliptical resulting in a slit like effect, stretching from top to bottom. This special ability allows a cat to squint its eyelids, covering only part of the pupil, affording him some manual control over the amount of light let in. Cat's pupils dilate much faster than human's, and also they can dilate three times larger. This allows them to allow in a lot of light which explains their extraordinary ability to see in low light conditions. They can't see very well in total darkness though which is somewhat of a misnomer.

Whiskers: Whiskers are an integral part of the cat's anatomy and. They have twenty-four movable whiskers in four sets on each upper lip on either side of its nose (some cats may have more). There are also a few on each cheek, tufts over the eyes, bristles on the chin, and on the back of the legs. Whiskers work as antennas and assist in navigation through narrow areas and let the cat know whether an opening is big enough for the body to pass through. Some cats have short whiskers or even none at all such as the Sphynx.

Whiskers also help in hunting. When a cat can't see its prey because it is too close to his face the whiskers move and form a basket shape around its muzzle in order to precisely detect the prey's location. Whiskers are also thought to help cats detect scents by directing air currents to the mouth and nose.

Nose: A cat's sense of smell is fourteen times stronger than a human's due to the nose being proportionally larger on a feline. A cat depends on its sense of smell for its survival and is probably more important than its sense of hearing in this regard. Cats use their sense of smell in several ways.

1: To smell food. From kitten hood a cat's heightened sense of smell will always direct him towards food and prey.

2: To locate a mate. Female cats on heat emit scents which are picked up by Toms from great distances. Females can also scent out a preferred mate by his territorial markings.

3: Warn against enemies and danger. Cats will often go outside looking alert, whiskers twitching and the nostrils wide open. This is done to look out for potential danger. He needs to know if he's safe before venturing out further. He needs to work out if that smell is just another cat or something more sinister.

4: Establishing territorial boundaries. Males often mark their territory with urine or scent from facial and feet glands. Other males will smell the markings and this will inform them that another cat's in the neighbourhood.

Paws: Cats have five toes on their front paws and four toes on their back feet. The paws are extremely sensitive and are filled with touch receptors and nerves. Cats feel vibrations through the pads on their feet. These pads are tough and are made from thick skin that serves to protect the foot and act as a shock absorber when jumping and landing. The paws consist of three sets of small bones that form a digit. These bones allow a cat to extend and retract his claws at will.

Teeth: Teeth are very important to a cat because they provide him with a quick and effective method to dispatch his prey. A kitten will have all his baby teeth in as little as eight weeks and a cat will have developed all its adult teeth by seven months. Owners should make sure they keep on top of their cat's dental hygiene to reduce the chances of tooth ache, gum disease and tooth decay.

Tail: Tails range from long and thin to short and thick. Cats use their tails as balancing poles and to keep their noses warm when they sleep.

Tongue: A cat's tongue feels very rough because it has backward-facing barbs (papillae) on it and they're the things that give the sandpaper sensation. The barbs make it easier for a cat to rasp the meat from the bones of his prey. They also also aid in grooming as they collect dirt, debris and loose hair from the cat's coat. The downside to the barbs is that anything the cat collects on his tongue will usually end up getting swallowed and that's how your cat may end up with hairballs.

Cats don't have as strong a sense of taste as humans but they can detect bitter, acidic and salty flavours however they can't detect sweet flavours which might go some way toward explaining why they generally don't like eating sweet foods.

USEFUL CAT CONTACTS

GLOBAL VETERINARY ASSOCIATIONS:

Australian Vet Association

PO box 371, Artarmon NSW 1570, Australia

Tel: (61) 2 9411 2733 www.ava.com.au

British small animal veterinary association

Woodrow house, 1 Telford way, Waterwells business park, Quedgeley, Gloucester, GL2 4AB

Tel: 01452 726 700 www.bsava.com

Federation of European Companion Animal Veterinary Associations

40 rue de berry, 75008 Paris, France

Tel: (33) 1 5383 9160 www.fecava.org

Irish Veterinary Association

53 Lansdowne Road, Ballsbridge, Dublin 4, Ireland

Tel: (353) 1 668 5263

Royal College of Veterinary Surgeons

www.rcvs.org.uk

BREED REGISTERIES:

Cat Fanciers' Association

www.cfainc.org

Governing Council of the Cat Fancy

Tel: 01278 427 575
http://ourworld.compuserve.com/homepages/GCCF_cats

The International Cat Association

www.tica.org

Traditional Cat Association

www.traditionalcats.com

WELFARE, RESEARCH AND GENERAL INTEREST:

Australian Cat Federation

PO Box 2151, Rosebud plaza, Victoria 3939, Australia

Tel: (61) 3 5986 1119 www.acf.asn.au

Cat's protection

www.cats.org.uk

Feline advisory bureau

Tel: 0870 742 2278 www.fabcats.org

RSPCA: Royal society for the prevention of cruelty to animals

Wilberforce way, Southwater, Horsham, West Sussex, RH13 RS

Tel: 0870 3335 999 www.rspca.org.au

RSPCA Australia:

PO box 265, Deakin West, Australian capital territory 2600, Australia

Tel: (61) 2 6282 8300 www.rspca.org.au

SSPCA: Scottish society

Braehead Mains, 603 Queensferry Road, Edinburgh EH4 6EA, Scotland

Tel: 0131 339 0222

USPCA: Ulster society

PO box 103, Belfast BT6 8US, Northern Ireland

Tel: 08000 28 00 10 www.uspca.co.uk

ISPCA: Irish society

300 Lower Rathmines road, Dublin 6, Ireland

Tel: (353) 1 497 7874 www.ispca.ie

Animal Aunts (Pet sitting agency)

Tel: 01730 821529 www.animalaunts.co.uk

Petlog: National microchip register

PO Box 2037, London W1A 1GP

Tel: 020 7518 1000 www.petlog.org.uk

The Winn Feline foundation

www.winnfelinehealth.org

Cat information and other helpful websites:

www.lib.uoguelph.ca/veterinary/vetfile

Information on microchips:

www.identichip.co.uk

A FEW FINAL WORDS BEFORE I GO AND FEED MY CATS

Thanks for reading my book I really appreciate it. If you liked it and found the information interesting and useful then please feel free to leave me a great review on Amazon.

I hope you enjoyed the book as much as I enjoyed writing it and that it will help not just first time cat owners but also people like me who have owned cats for many years.

Whatever cat you decide to go for don't forget that if you love him, care for him and give him lots of attention then you will have his unconditional love for the rest of your very long and happy time together.

Good luck!

Sally

Printed in Great Britain
by Amazon.co.uk, Ltd.,
Marston Gate.